What Is Biblical Wisdom?

Crucial Questions booklets provide a quick introduction to definitive Christian truths. This expanding collection includes titles such as:

Who Is Jesus?

Can I Trust the Bible?

Does Prayer Change Things?

Can I Know God's Will?

How Should I Live in This World?

What Does It Mean to Be Born Again?

Can I Be Sure I'm Saved?

What Is Faith?

What Can I Do with My Guilt?

What Is the Trinity?

TO BROWSE THE REST OF THE SERIES,
PLEASE VISIT: LIGONIER.ORG/CQ

CQ

What Is Biblical Wisdom?

R.C. SPROUL

 LIGONIER MINISTRIES

What Is Biblical Wisdom?
© 2020 by R.C. Sproul

Published by Ligonier Ministries
421 Ligonier Court, Sanford, FL 32771
Ligonier.org

Printed in China
RR Donnelley
0001121
First edition

ISBN 978-1-64289-234-5 (Paperback)
ISBN 978-1-64289-235-2 (ePub)
ISBN 978-1-64289-236-9 (Kindle)

Cover design: Ligonier Creative
Interior typeset: Katherine Lloyd, The DESK

Unless otherwise indicated, Scripture quotations are from the ESV ® Bible (The Holy Bible, English Standard Version ®), copyright © 2001 by Crossway, a publishing ministry of Good News Publishers. Used by permission. All rights reserved.

The Library of Congress has cataloged the Reformation Trust edition as follows:
Names: Sproul, R. C. (Robert Charles), 1939-2017, author.
Title: What is biblical wisdom? / R.C. Sproul.
Description: Orlando, FL : Reformation Trust Publishing, a division of
  Ligonier Ministries, [2020]
Identifiers: LCCN 2019035545 (print) | LCCN 2019035546 (ebook) |
  ISBN 9781642892345 (paperback) | ISBN 9781642892352 (epub) |
  ISBN 9781642892369 (kindle edition)
Subjects: LCSH: Wisdom literature--Criticism, interpretation, etc. | Bible.
  Psalms--Criticism, interpretation, etc.
Classification: LCC BS1455 .S69 2020 (print) | LCC BS1455 (ebook) | DDC
  223/.06--dc23
LC record available at https://lccn.loc.gov/2019035545
LC ebook record available at https://lccn.loc.gov/2019035546

Contents

Chapter One

Introduction to Wisdom

As a college student, I majored in the academic discipline of philosophy. On the first day, in the very first philosophy course that I took, the professor wrote the word *philosophy* on the board. He then broke it down into its etymological derivation. *Philosophy* comes from the Greek, and of course, the Greeks are usually seen as the founding fathers of Western philosophy—first with the pre-Socratic philosophers; then with Socrates himself; followed by Plato, Aristotle, and others.

The word *philosophy* combines two important Greek words: the first part of the word comes from the Greek *phileō*, which means "to love." We are familiar with this word in the English language because we all know the meaning of the city of Philadelphia—the city of brotherly love.

Some may also be familiar with this word from Jesus' conversation with Peter in John 21, where Jesus repeatedly asks Peter, "Do you love me?" (vv. 15–17). In this exchange, the New Testament uses two different words that are both translated by the English word *love*. The first is *agapē*, which is the spiritual love, the zenith of love, the kind of love that God sheds abroad in our hearts through the Holy Spirit. And there is also *philia*, which is used for brotherly love and affection. This is the word that was joined here to the word *philosophy*.

The second part of the word *philosophy* comes from another Greek word, *sophia*, which is the word for "wisdom." When you combine these words, *philia* and *sophia*, the simple meaning of the term *philosophy* is "the love of wisdom." This intrigued me as a college student in my first course in the study of philosophy because I naturally assumed that by studying philosophy I would learn all about wisdom in a practical sense.

However, I soon discovered that Greek philosophy, for example, focused on abstract, weighty questions in metaphysics (the study of ultimate being) and epistemology (the study of the process by which human beings learn). It is true that historically in the discipline of philosophy, one of its subdivisions is ethics—particularly, the science of normative ethics, which is the study of imperatives on how one ought to live. And normative ethics was certainly a concern of the ancient Greeks.

Socrates was convinced that proper conduct, or right living, is intimately connected with right knowledge. That is, for a person to behave in a courageous manner, he must first understand what courage is and what courage means. So, Socrates was convinced that philosophy was not just an unrelated, impractical, abstract discipline of human speculation but very much concerned with concrete daily living. He was concerned about the decadence of Greek civilization in his day, and he saw that the Greek culture was in the process of disintegration because it had lost its moral foundation.

It's amazing how many parallels there are between the Greece of Socrates' day and America of today. So many of the same crises are being visited. But despite Socrates' concern for ethics, Plato's penetrating research into the idea of the good, and Aristotle's full volume on the science of ethics, when we think of philosophy today, for the most part we think of the other areas—the speculative investigation into metaphysics and epistemology.

When we come to the Wisdom Literature of the Old Testament, we see a completely different emphasis on the pursuit of wisdom among the Jews compared to the Greeks. When we speak of the Wisdom Literature of the Old Testament, we're referring to the group of books that includes Psalms, Proverbs, Ecclesiastes, Song of Solomon, and Job. The Wisdom Literature was understood as a special kind of literature among the Jewish people in the ancient world. There are obvious differences between the dramatic narrative of Job, the love song of the Song of Solomon, the prayers of the Psalter, and the aphorisms of Proverbs; nevertheless, a single motif carries through this entire body of literature that we call wisdom.

It has been said of Greek philosophy that the assertion that there is one God who is sovereign over all creation was a very late development in the pursuit of philosophy among the ancient Greeks, that it was, in a sense, the conclusion of their philosophy rather than something that was manifested early on in their search for truth. By contrast, for the Jew with his sacred Scriptures, the very first line of the Old Testament says, "In the beginning, God created the heavens and the earth" (Gen. 1:1). There is no attempt on the first page of Genesis to offer any argument, reason, or proof for the existence of God. It simply starts with the statement about the God who is God over all creation. Monotheism isn't the end of the trail as it was for the Greeks; it's at the very beginning of the sacred writings of the Jews.

One of the reasons the Jews did not feel constrained to give speculative arguments for the existence of God is that they were convinced that God had already quite ably done the job Himself: "The heavens declare the glory of God, and the sky above proclaims his handiwork" (Ps. 19:1). The question that concerned the Jew was not whether there is a God but rather *who* that God is. What is His name? What is His nature and character? And the whole of the Old Testament focuses on God's self-disclosure—the unveiling of His character, His person, and His nature to His covenant people.

The body of literature that we find in the middle of the Old Testament called the Wisdom Literature affirms again and again that "the fear of the LORD is the beginning of wisdom" (Ps. 111:10; cf. Prov. 1:7; 9:10). For the Jew, wisdom meant an understanding, practically speaking, of how to live a life that is pleasing to God. It was the pursuit of godliness that was the central concern of the writers of Hebrew Wisdom Literature. And they say at the very beginning that the absolute, foundational, necessary condition for anyone to have true wisdom is that he must first possess and cultivate a fear of the Lord.

This fear is not the terror that a prisoner in a concentration camp experiences every time he hears the footsteps of his torturer. Martin Luther called it a filial fear. It's the fear of a child who is in awe of his father and doesn't want to do anything that would violate his father and disrupt their loving relationship. This fear consists of reverence, awe, and respect. When the wisdom writer says that the fear of the Lord is the beginning of wisdom, he is saying this: If we want to acquire actual wisdom, the absolute, essential starting point at which we begin and continue that quest is in a posture of reverence and adoration for God.

By contrast, David tells us that "the fool says in his heart, 'There is no God'" (Ps. 14:1). Wisdom is constantly being contrasted with foolishness. We must understand that in Hebrew literature, the term *fool* or *foolish* does not describe a person who lacks intelligence. To be foolish to the Jew is not necessarily to be stupid—a person could be erudite, extremely learned, and still be called a fool. One of the harshest judgments that we could receive from the mouth of Christ is to be called a fool. He told a parable of the rich fool who had great prosperity and was preoccupied with the quest for riches, saying, "I will tear down my barns and build larger ones" (Luke 12:18). God said to that man: "Fool! This night your soul is required of you" (v. 20).

According to the Bible, to be called a fool is to be deemed irreligious and godless. The fool is the person who has no respect or reverence for God, and when someone does not have any reverence for God or adoration in his heart toward Him, his life will inevitably show it.

We also see that the Wisdom Literature of the Old Testament makes a clear and sharp distinction between wisdom and knowledge. They are not the same, for even the most learned people and the most sophisticated scholars do foolish things. A person can have unbounded knowledge but not have wisdom. Sometimes we are educated beyond our intelligence to the point that we haven't quite grasped the fruit of concrete living despite the knowledge that we have been able to acquire.

It has been said by secular commentators that twentieth-century civilization experienced an unprecedented explosion of knowledge along with an unprecedented period of violence and moral decay. Humanity has tamed its universe—we can go to the moon, cure diseases, and build powerful computers—but we can't tame the impulses of our own hearts. We have acquired knowledge, but we lack wisdom. And the Wisdom Literature teaches that we can possess knowledge yet never have wisdom.

However, the reverse is not the case—we cannot have wisdom without knowledge. The anti-intellectual spirit of our times would rejoice in the proposition that we don't need to study the Bible or theology—that all we need is a personal relationship with Jesus. But that faulty conclusion is on a collision course with what the Wisdom Literature teaches. The Wisdom Literature says: Get knowledge, but above all, get wisdom. The purpose for learning the things of God is the acquisition of wisdom—we can't have wisdom without knowledge. Ignorance breeds foolishness, but the knowledge that we must pursue to gain this wisdom that is more precious than rubies and pearls is the knowledge of God.

The writers of the Wisdom Literature understood this principle: there can be no real human wisdom until we first know the character of God. For the Jew, wisdom meant living a life that is pleasing to God. How can we know how to live in a way that pleases God if we don't know the God we're trying to please? Far from repudiating knowledge, the Wisdom Literature places knowledge in its proper perspective. The same kind of thought is found in the New Testament, where we read that "'knowledge' puffs up, but love builds up" (1 Cor. 8:1). We can have knowledge and become proud and arrogant in our knowledge, lacking the love of God. But these are not either/or—we must have knowledge *and* wisdom, knowledge *and* love, not an ignorant love or an ignorant wisdom.

Proverbs 8 contains a magnificent poetic expression of the nature of wisdom in which wisdom itself is personified. It begins: "Does not wisdom call? Does not understanding raise her voice?" (v. 1). And in verses 22–24, we read these words: "The LORD possessed me at the beginning of his work, the first of his acts of old. Ages ago I was set up, at the first, before the beginning of the earth. When there were no depths I was brought forth." In poetic expression, we are told that before God ever created the world, He had from all eternity, within Himself, His own personal wisdom. The first thing that God expressed before He even expressed Himself in creation was this eternal, divine wisdom.

The Apostle Paul, in the New Testament, links this wisdom to Christ, who is called "the wisdom of God" (1 Cor. 1:24). If there is a link between the Wisdom Literature of the Old Testament and the teachings of the New Testament, it is that the wisdom of God points us to the absolute wisdom of God—Christ Himself.

Can you remember as a child being asked what you wanted to be when you grew up? How did you answer? When I was asked that question as a child, I said I wanted to play baseball for the Pittsburgh Pirates. What was your driving ambition or your main aspiration? I have rarely, if ever, met someone who would answer that question by saying, "I want to be wise." We want to be rich, successful, famous, and comfortable. We do not live in a day and age that puts a high value on wisdom. But in Old Testament Israel, life was hard and life seemed cruel. Simply surviving required a certain element of wisdom. Solomon, for example, was so extolled for his wisdom that even the queen of Sheba journeyed just to learn from his wisdom. Yet today, we won't even travel as far as across the street to gain wisdom. We neglect God's Word, which is the supreme textbook of all wisdom. And in that regard, we have become fools.

Chapter Two

The Nature
of Wisdom

It's always distressing to me when I hear people say, "I would like to read the Bible, but every time I try, I just don't understand it. It's too deep for me." The Bible, for the most part, is not written in technical, philosophical language that requires a special degree before one can understand it. In fact, one of the great principles of the Reformation was the view of the basic clarity of Scripture. That is, its central message is so clearly and simply set forth in so many places that a child can understand what is necessary to know for faith and life in the presence of God.

At the same time, we must recognize that not all Scripture is equally clear. There are some sections that are profoundly difficult to understand, and it can be helpful to learn how to recognize certain forms and patterns in Scripture that enable us to more easily discern the point of the text. The Bible is not just a storybook. It contains historical narrative, poetry, parables, letters, and highly imaginative symbolic literature (called apocalyptic literature, such as the book of Revelation or the book of Daniel). These different styles, or forms, of Scripture require certain basic rules of interpretation in order to understand them correctly.

Our particular focus is Wisdom Literature, which is in large measure communicated through poetry. We are familiar with poetry in our own language and culture. We have different kinds of poetry: short poems, long poems, epic poems. We have poems that rhyme and poems that don't rhyme. One of the classic characteristics of our poetry—and of poetry found around the world—is its metered structure. There are so many beats to a line, just like a piece of music. There is almost a cadence, where the syllables are arranged in such a way that the emphasis falls in a mathematically proportionate way.

The Jews, however, had another technique that they used in poetry that was highly significant. It is important to understand what this technique is and how to recognize it because it is almost like a key that unlocks hidden treasures from the cave of sacred Scripture. That particular technique or literary device is called *parallelism*. As we understand from mathematics, things that are parallel go side by side in the same direction. There are different kinds of parallelisms found in the Wisdom Literature of the Bible, and it is important to note that they are not found exclusively in those books that we call Wisdom Literature. They are found throughout Scripture, including in the prophecies of Isaiah and even in the teachings of Jesus in the New Testament.

While there are many different types of parallelism, there are three main kinds seen in the Scriptures, particularly in the Wisdom Literature. The first is *synonymous parallelism*. This is seen when the same idea is expressed in two consecutive lines, but the wording is different. In other words, the writer uses different words to say the same thing.

One of the most familiar examples of this type of parallelism is found in the Aaronic benediction: "The LORD bless you and keep you; the LORD make his face to shine upon you and be gracious to you; the LORD lift up his countenance upon you and give you peace" (Num. 6:24–26). In this example, there are three lines, and each line contains two ideas. The first line says, "The LORD bless you and keep you." The next line has that same couplet, but with different words. The first part, "the LORD make his face to shine upon you," means the same thing as "May He bless you." And the second part, "be gracious to you," is virtually the same as "keep you." The final line, "the LORD lift up his countenance upon you and give you peace," reiterates what the first and second lines say. They are synonymous.

Why is it important to recognize this type of parallelism when we see it? Sometimes when we are reading Scripture, we may understand what one line means but be puzzled by the meaning of the second line (or, if it contains more lines of parallelism, the third line). If we understand the meaning of at least one line and realize that parallelism is being used, that is the key to unlock the door. If the meaning of one line is clear to us, then we know the lines that are difficult to understand mean essentially the same thing using different words.

Consider the Lord's Prayer. When Jesus taught His disciples how to pray, He made this statement: "And lead us not into temptation, but deliver us from evil" (Matt. 6:13). This can be confusing to many people because the book of James teaches, "Let no one say when he is tempted, 'I am being tempted by God,' for God cannot be tempted with evil, and he himself tempts no one" (1:13). God doesn't tempt anyone in the sense of luring or enticing him to sin. That would cast a shadow on the holiness of God. If the Bible looks askance at such an idea, why would Jesus say, "Lead us not into temptation"?

This apparent contradiction is clarified when we read the next line of the Lord's Prayer, which amplifies the request of "lead us not into temptation" by saying "but deliver us from evil" (Matt. 6:13). The word that is commonly used in Greek to refer to evil is *ponēros*. When the Bible uses this term in the abstract, it occurs in the neuter gender, *ponēron*. But in the Lord's Prayer, when Jesus says "but deliver us from evil," He doesn't use the neuter gender form of *ponēros*. Instead, He uses the masculine form with the definite article "the." Thus, a more accurate translation would be this: "And lead us not into temptation, but deliver us from *the evil one*." *Ponēros* is a frequent designation in Scripture for Satan.

During His earthly life, Jesus was driven by the Holy Spirit into the wilderness for the purpose of being put to the test (Matt. 4:1–11). Jesus was isolated and exposed to the full assault of Satan. The *ponēros* came to attack Him, but His mission was to pass the test, conquer Satan, and win the victory—not only for Himself, but for those for whom He would die to redeem. In the Lord's Prayer, Jesus is essentially saying: "My Father put Me to the test. My Father asked Me to go and wrestle for forty days and forty nights with the unbridled assault of Satan. When you pray, pray that you would be spared from that." To ask the Father not to lead us into temptation is to say: "Father, don't send me to the place of testing or ask me to bear that kind of difficulty. Instead, deliver me from *ponēros*, the evil one." And we would miss all of that if we didn't recognize the presence of parallelism in the text.

Another kind of parallelism, even more common, is called *antithetical parallelism*. When a thesis or proposition is given, the viewpoint that challenges, contrasts with, or denies that thesis is called the *antithesis*—it speaks against the original thesis. Antithetical parallelism occurs when statements are made together but are in direct contrast with each other. The same message is being communicated in antithetical parallelism just as in synonymous parallelism. The difference is that the poetic form of antithetical parallelism sets up the idea in terms of a positive statement followed by its negative rejection.

For example, Proverbs 10:1 says, "A wise son makes a glad father, but a foolish son is a sorrow to his mother." This is an antithesis, or contrast. A wise son brings joy and gladness to the parent, but the foolish son brings grief to the parent. Verse 2 contains another example of antithetical parallelism: "Treasures gained by wickedness do not profit, but righteousness delivers from death." Do you see the contrast? Verse 3 contains yet another example: "The LORD does not let the righteous go hungry, but he thwarts the craving of the wicked." Psalm 1 provides another example of antithetical parallelism by contrasting the godly man, who is like a tree planted by streams of water bringing forth fruit, with the wicked, who are like chaff that the wind drives away.

Proverbs 11:1 says, "A false balance is an abomination to the LORD, but a just weight is his delight." God's wisdom in the Proverbs is not just cute aphorisms. In

Proverbs, we learn principles of righteousness and justice that affect how we do business. Here we have a warning against unjust weights and measures so that we might not cheat our neighbor but instead deal honestly with him.

One biblical text that many have found confusing, particularly in older translations, is Isaiah 45:7. It reads, "I form light and create darkness; I make well-being and create calamity; I am the LORD, who does all these things." This passage may appear to be teaching that God is the author of evil—that He creates evil. And if that's true, that would make God evil. However, there are about eight different words that can be translated as "evil" in Hebrew. And if we read carefully, we can recognize that antithetical parallelism is being employed in this passage. Notice the first line: "I form light and create darkness." Light and darkness are set in contrast to each other. The next statement says, "I make well-being and create calamity." Another way of saying that would be, "I bring prosperity and bring judgment." This passage has nothing to do with God's doing something that is morally evil, and that is perfectly clear if we recognize the presence of antithetical parallelism in the text.

One last example of antithetical parallelism is found in Proverbs 28:1, which says, "The wicked flee when no one pursues, but the righteous are bold as a lion." Scripture often contrasts the wise man and the fool, the righteous person and the godless person, and the difference is displayed in strikingly vivid images. The unrighteous person flees when no one pursues. He trembles at the rustling of a leaf. This is characteristic of the lifestyle of those with a guilty conscience. But the righteous—those who are free from a conscience that's paralyzing them and frightening them—are bold as the lion. It's a marvelous contrast.

The third form of parallelism is *synthetic parallelism*, which contains a buildup from one level to the next. For example, Proverbs 6:16–19 says, "There are six things that the LORD hates, seven that are an abomination to him: haughty eyes, a lying tongue, and hands that shed innocent blood, a heart that devises wicked plans, feet that make haste to run to evil, a false witness who breathes out lies, and one who sows discord among brothers." This passage builds toward a crescendo as it lists a number of specific sins that God hates.

As we look for these forms of parallelism when we read Scripture, we will find a key that unlocks a treasure chest. As we note synonymous, antithetical, and synthetic parallelism in the Wisdom Literature, we will much more fully understand the written Word of God.

Chapter Three

The Psalms

As we reflect on our years of schooling, most of us have a favorite teacher who comes to mind. My favorite teacher was my seminary professor Dr. John Gerstner. I devoured everything he wrote and have listened to hundreds of hours of his lectures. One thing I noticed is that when I listened intently to him as he was working through a carefully planned argument, I could think along with him and would often know what he was going to say before he said it—I could anticipate not just the general idea but the very words that he would use. Perhaps you've also had that kind of experience with people with whom you're very familiar. You can almost finish their sentences for them.

Another thing I discovered over all those years of listening to him is that there were moments when I was absolutely sure of what he was going to say next, but then he hit me with a curveball and said something totally unexpected. This same thing happens sometimes when we're reading the New Testament and listening to the teachings of Jesus, our supreme mentor. We read the Gospel accounts over and over again, and we begin to grasp the flow of Jesus' thinking. After all, our goal is to have the mind of Christ. We ought to not only think His thoughts after Him but also be able to anticipate what our Lord would say in a given circumstance.

However, there's one place in the New Testament that surprises me so often. The disciples come to Jesus after having observed the power that is manifest in Him. They see the extraordinary passion and level of communication that He has with the Father in His prayer life, and the disciples link these two together. They conclude that there must be a connection between His powerful prayer life and the manifestation of power in His ministry. So when they come to

Him, they don't say, "Lord, teach us how to walk on water" or "Teach us how to turn water into wine." Instead, they want to get to the very root, and so they make this request: "Lord, teach us how to pray."

Think about this for a moment. What would you expect Jesus to say in response to them? No matter how many times I've read this passage and how much I know what's coming, I'm still surprised at Jesus' answer. He says, "Pray then like this: Our Father in heaven, hallowed be your name" (Matt. 6:9). Then He gives His disciples the model prayer. Far be it from me to criticize the Lord in the answer He gives to His disciples, but it does surprise me. What I would have expected Jesus to say to His disciples in that moment is this: "If you want to learn how to pray, immerse yourselves in the Psalms of the Old Testament." If you were to ask me, "Teach me how to pray," the answer I would give is, "If you really want to learn how to pray, spend hour after hour in the Psalms."

In the 1960s, something unique in the history of Christianity erupted in the United States: the charismatic movement. Before the '60s, the movement had been contained in certain small denominations, but then suddenly, there was an explosion of interest in the gifts of the Holy Spirit. It swept through the Roman Catholic Church and mainline Protestant denominations and became a historical phenomenon. At the heart of charismatic interest at that time was the experience of *glossolalia*—speaking or praying in tongues.

Many people came to me in those days earnestly seeking the ability to pray in tongues. As we talked, I frequently asked this question: "Why do you want to be able to pray in tongues?" I got the same response time after time. People would say: "I want something that will enrich my prayer life. I feel so inarticulate, so inadequate, so unable to express the way I feel in the depths of my soul when I'm on my knees. If I could get some kind of Holy Spirit–inspired means of communicating with God, that would be glorious." These people had a profound desire to go to another level of communication with God, and many of my friends became deeply immersed in the charismatic movement. We want to have the words on our tongues to express how we really feel toward God.

There are various aspects to prayer, including thanksgiving, confession, supplication, and adoration. The place where our vocabulary fails us the most is in the area of adoration. In the sixteenth century, John Calvin wrote a response to the critics who were complaining about his doctrine (specifically, his doctrine of providence). In his response, Calvin used a particular expression over and over again. He said something to this effect: "Why are you complaining about the inscrutable ways of our adorable God?" It struck me how often Calvin referred to God as "our adorable God." We tend to use the word *adorable* as a synonym for *cute*, but Calvin, like many of the other Reformers, was trying to capture the profound sense of adoration we ought to feel for the greatness and the glory of God. If there's anything that is characteristically missing from modern evangelicalism, it is that preoccupation with the adoration of the greatness of God. We're defective in our understanding of God's character.

What does this have to do with Wisdom Literature? Remember that Wisdom Literature is given to instruct us in living lives that are pleasing to God. The Psalms might not dispense practical guidance as the book of Proverbs does, for instance, but it does help with living a God-glorifying life. The book of Psalms is made up of different types of prayers and hymns, and at its heart is a spirit of adoration. The reason I tell people to immerse themselves in the Psalms if they want to learn how to pray is that in the Psalms we have divinely inspired prayers.

In Romans, Paul teaches that when we come before God in prayer, God the Holy Spirit is working to assist us in expressing our thoughts before Him. He intercedes for us with groans that are unutterable. But in the Psalms, we have divinely inspired prayers: prayers of supplication, prayers of celebration, prayers of confession, and above all, prayers of adoration. When David prayed in adoration before God, he was not inarticulate. The Holy Spirit knows how we should pray, and He assists us in expressing ourselves to God in prayer.

In Psalm 8, David prays this:

O Lord, our Lord,
     how majestic is your name in all the earth!
You have set your glory above the heavens.
     Out of the mouth of babies and infants,
you have established strength because of your foes,
     to still the enemy and the avenger.

When I look at your heavens, the work of your fingers,
     the moon and the stars, which you have set in place,
what is man that you are mindful of him,
     and the son of man that you care for him?

Yet you have made him a little lower than the heavenly
    beings
    and crowned him with glory and honor.
You have given him dominion over the works of
    your hands;
    you have put all things under his feet,
all sheep and oxen,
    and also the beasts of the field,
the birds of the heavens, and the fish of the sea,
    whatever passes along the paths of the seas.

O Lord, our Lord,
    how majestic is your name in all the earth!

Under the supervision of God the Holy Spirit, David
pours out his soul in the adoration and exaltation of the
majesty of God. Wouldn't we all like to be able to pray
like this? In the writings of the great saints of the ages—
even though their writings are not inspired by the Holy
Spirit as the book of Psalms was—we find a similar pattern
of expression of a spirit of reverence, awe, and adoration
for God. One historian observed that every time we see in
the record of church history a large and significant revival

of the people of God, we also see a renewed interest in the Psalms because there's something about the Psalter that induces the soul to worship. There can't be genuine revival unless it is followed by a heightened sense of worship among the people of God. The book of Psalms gives us undiluted worship—worship that we know is pleasing to God because it comes to us from His wisdom and from His own inspiration.

One of the hardest things to do is to express our sorrow when we are deeply hurt or grieved. When someone has died, many people struggle with knowing what to say to the person's loved ones. They feel inadequate to express compassion, grief, or mourning. They fear that any words they use will seem empty, vacuous, and trite. But we do have words that guide us in what to say in these moments, and we find them in the Psalms.

We find not only psalms of adoration but also psalms that express the broken heart of the sinner who comes in profound contrition before God. David not only knew how to praise God, but he also knew how to repent before God and confess his sins before God. He knew how to express his own mourning and grief: "I am weary with my moaning; every night I flood my bed with tears; I drench my couch with my weeping" (Ps. 6:6). While the prayers in the book of Psalms celebrate many great things about God, they are not sermons about God. Rather, they are communications to God.

True prayer comes from the heart. It's not just an expression of phrases or carefully devised sentences. Prayer is a tender moment of a soul speaking to God directly. When we hear others pray like that, there's almost a sense that we're violating their privacy.

So we should read the Psalms not just to gain a better vocabulary and become more articulate in our prayers but also to learn the spirit of prayer. This spirit of prayer is there in the broken heart of David. It's there in the joyous celebration of God's people when they celebrate deliverance. It's even there in the most problematic of the psalms, the so-called imprecatory psalms, in which the psalmist calls down the wrath of God on his enemies.

In Psalm 139:21–22, David makes a statement that is difficult to understand. He says: "Do I not hate those who hate you, O Lord? And do I not loathe those who rise up against you? I hate them with complete hatred; I count them my enemies." If Jesus calls us to love our enemies, then how can David hate God's enemies with complete hatred? What is the nature of this hatred? Does complete hatred mean pure hate that is undiluted by charity? If that's the case, then the Holy Spirit is recording David's sin in this verse.

Or does David mean that there is a kind of antipathy that is legitimate to have toward the enemies of the kingdom of God? We are to pray for the well-being of all, including our enemies. Yet at the same time, we pray for the defeat of God's enemies. To give an example, a person could pray for the soul of Adolf Hitler while at the same time praying that he would be stopped in his madness. But even in these prayers of judgment and anger, we find the heart of God.

We look to the book of Psalms as our model of wisdom in prayer. As we daily immerse ourselves in the Psalms, the sacred literature of prayer and adoration contained in it will begin to run through the fiber of our lives.

Chapter Four

Proverbs

Every culture has its own unique collected wisdom that has accumulated over the centuries. These insights of the wise are usually preserved in the form of the proverb. In American culture, we have *Poor Richard's Almanack*, produced by Benjamin Franklin, which contains homespun wisdom encapsulated in short, pithy statements that we call proverbs. Many of these sayings have endured even to today, such as "Lost time is never found again" and "Early to bed and early to rise makes a man healthy, wealthy, and wise."

As a child, I never understood the proverb "A penny saved is a penny earned." It wasn't until later in life—when I learned the law of compound interest—that I began to understand the saying. In fact, I remember once going to the barbershop, and the woman cutting my hair started talking to me about the state lottery. She told me that she bought lottery tickets every single day, and she told me how much they cost. I was amazed at how much money this woman was spending on lottery tickets.

She asked me if I played the lottery, and I said, "No." She asked, "Why not?" I said, "I can't afford it." She thought I was joking, so while she finished cutting my hair, I sat with a pencil and paper and did some rough calculations. When I finished, I turned to her and said: "Let me ask you a question. Suppose that right now I gave you a check for sixty thousand dollars. Would you go out and spend that sixty thousand dollars on lottery tickets?" She said: "No, absolutely not. I have all kinds of other things I'd like to do." I said: "Well, I just did these computations taking what you spend on lottery tickets every day and took it out over a period of twenty years. If you invested this money at a reasonable rate of return, after twenty years you would have sixty thousand dollars." She couldn't believe it. She hadn't yet learned that a penny saved is a penny earned. The wise person is one who earns interest on his money, not the one who pays interest on his money.

How do we approach the biblical book of Proverbs? How do proverbs function, particularly when we find them among the writings of the Wisdom Literature of the Old Testament? If every culture has its collection of sayings that preserves the insights of the ages, then what makes the book of Proverbs in the Old Testament different from all other such collections? The difference is that they are inspired by God. They find their origin in the mind of God and reflect supernatural and divine wisdom—not just the insights of crafty people in this world.

Because the biblical proverbs are inspired, some people make the mistake of assuming that a proverb is like a law—that is, that it imposes a universal obligation. As a result, they treat the proverbs as if they were a list of divine commandments. However, this view leads to problems because that is not the function of a proverb, and that is not the form in which the book of Proverbs comes to us. Even divinely inspired proverbs reflect what we would call truisms or insights that are *generally* true and that apply to many concrete life situations but not necessarily to *all* life situations.

To illustrate, consider the American cultural proverb "Look before you leap." This is good insight and a valuable truism to keep in mind in life. But we also have another proverb that says, "He who hesitates is lost." If in every life situation we tried to apply both of these proverbs at the same time, it would result in much confusion.

I remember as a teenager sleeping in a tent one summer night with my friends. It was about 2 a.m. and I couldn't sleep. Since I didn't have a curfew and I wasn't at home with my parents, I started roaming the streets of our town. I wasn't doing anything illegal. I was just loafing and walking up and down the streets. I then saw a car coming up the street and immediately recognized it—the town police car. The last thing I wanted was to have the police officer stop me and say: "What are you doing out at two o'clock in the morning? Do your parents know you're out here?" So I reacted by instinct and started to run.

The car stopped, and I heard the door open. The police officer got out and started yelling and chasing me. He was chasing me at full speed, and I was running as fast as I could, trying to put distance between us. I started running through someone's backyard, and I came to a very high hedge. I had no idea what was on the other side of the hedge—it could have dropped off the edge of a cliff for all I knew. But I knew what was behind me—the policeman coming as fast as he could—and I had no opportunity to look before I leaped. All I knew was that he who hesitates is lost, and if I stopped, I was going to be caught by the police. So I just kept running, dove headfirst through the hedge, and landed in a child's sandbox in someone's yard.

It made a great deal of noise, and the lights came on in the house. Shades rolled up and windows were opened. I picked myself up out of the sandbox and just kept on running. The policeman never did catch me. I learned in that situation the wisdom of not hesitating. That was a life situation in which I could not afford to hesitate. But at the same time, I also learned the peril of leaping without looking.

This illustrates the point that in many of life's circumstances and situations, wisdom dictates that we examine carefully where we're going to place our next steps so that we are not just running blindly. At the same time, we can't be paralyzed to such a degree with our judgments, analysis, and evaluation that we lose opportunities when they present themselves. That is what is encapsulated in the idea of "He who hesitates is lost."

It isn't bothersome, theologically, to find proverbs that conflict in their advice in our own cultural wisdom. But when we find them in the Bible, it can raise questions about the trustworthiness of Scripture. For example, the book of Proverbs says, "Answer not a fool according to his folly" (26:4). But in the very next verse we read, "Answer a fool according to his folly" (v. 5). This jumps right off the page as a seeming contradiction. How can we incorporate this wisdom into our lives when on one hand it tells us not to answer a fool according to his folly and on the other hand, to answer a fool according to his folly? How can both be statements of wisdom?

This is similar to the conflict between "Look before you leap" and "He who hesitates is lost." There are certain circumstances in which it would not be wise to answer a fool according to his folly, and there are other circumstances in which it would be wise to answer a fool according to his folly. For example, take the proverb that says, "Answer not a fool according to his folly." The idea is that if someone is speaking utter foolishness, it's not generally wise to engage in that kind of foolish discussion. The discussion will not be fruitful and is a waste of time, both for the fool who starts it and for the fool who carries it on. We all know that there are certain circumstances where we're better off not saying anything so that we can avoid any deep discussion with people who are talking in a foolish manner.

But when is it appropriate to answer a fool according to his folly? One of the most effective ways of arguing—understood by the Hebrews and found in biblical teaching—was also made an art form by the ancient Greek philosophers. It is the use of the argument called the *reductio ad absurdum*. The philosopher Zeno of Elea was the master of this particular technique of debate. In this form of argumentation, a person reduces his opponent's argument to absurdity, arguing from his premise in a hypothetical way. One might say to his opponent, "Oh, you say such and such? Well, let me take that position, and if what you say is true, then this would also be true." And then the person shows his opponent the necessary logical conclusion that flows out of his opponent's argument, showing that if his opponent is consistent with his premise, that premise will lead to an absurd conclusion. In that sense, when the fool makes a foolish premise and gives a foolish argument, it can be very effective to answer the fool according to his folly by stepping onto his grounds and saying, "OK, I'll take your position for the sake of argument, and I'm going to take it to its logical conclusion and show you the fool-ishness of it."

Apart from these proverbs that show different responses for different situations, the book of Proverbs is for the most part concerned with giving practical guidelines for daily experience. Here's one example. In my early Christian days, I was trying to drive home from Pittsburgh, and I had to go through a long tunnel outside the city. The police are very strict about which lanes cars can be in while in the tunnels, and crossing between lanes is not allowed. I realized that I was in the wrong lane, and when I came out of the tunnel, I would have to make a left turn. I was in the right lane, and there was only about a hundred yards between the end of the tunnel and the traffic light to turn left.

As soon as I got out of the tunnel, I darted from the right lane into the left lane. Unfortunately, just as I did that, the light turned red, and I had to stop. I had made that move right in front of a policeman who was sitting on the back of a motorcycle. I looked in the rearview mir-ror, and I saw this policeman. His face was red. He got off his motorcycle and started running toward my car, and I thought I was in trouble. He came and literally pounded on the roof of my car, and I rolled down the window.

When I looked at him, he screamed, "What do you think you're doing?" And the first words that came into my mind were from the book of Proverbs: "A soft answer turns away wrath" (15:1). I looked at him and said: "Sir, I'm very sorry. I know that what I did was wrong, and I shouldn't have done it. I'm sorry." This caught him completely off guard. He was ready for an argument, and when I responded gently, he looked at me, shook his head, and said, "Forget it." He turned around and walked away. The book of Proverbs is incredibly practical.

The book of Proverbs is a treasure trove of wisdom and insight for guiding our lives. One of its recurring themes is industry. We often forget that one of the most basic sins that besets us in life is slothfulness, or laziness. But Proverbs enjoins us before God to be people who are diligent and industrious in our labor. So often, clever allusions are made to the animal kingdom. For example, the ant is used as an illustration of a good worker: "Go to the ant, O sluggard" (6:6). We should learn wisdom from the ant who works so hard to prepare the provisions for its group. At other times, Proverbs compares people to inanimate objects: "As a door turns on its hinges, so does a sluggard on his bed" (26:14).

Yet at the same time, in contrast, Proverbs tells us, "Whoever works his land will have plenty of bread" (28:19). Those who work hard know the rewards and satisfaction that come from a full day's work. There is then a certain sweetness that comes when we enjoy the fruits of our labor and when we finally can rest—a sweetness that is absent if we procrastinate and then toss and turn on our beds. We have an uneasy conscience because we haven't been diligent that day.

Proverbs is a depository of treasure with all kinds of applications for daily life. It contains concrete pieces of advice that come from the mind of God Himself. If we want wisdom, this is a fountain from which to drink. It has untold riches for our consumption and edification, and he who is hungry will eat of these morsels. He who is foolish will not.

If we are really thinking in biblical categories, we will find ourselves out of step with most of the world. We need to listen to the wisdom of God so that we can cut through the cacophony of noise that would lead us into all kinds of confusion about life. Refresh your mind, spend time in Proverbs, and seek the wisdom of God.

Chapter Five

Ecclesiastes, Job, and the Song of Solomon

In addition to Psalms and Proverbs, the books of Ecclesiastes, Job, and the Song of Solomon are generally classified under the heading of Wisdom Literature. I have often said that I'm convinced I'm the only person in the history of the Christian church who was converted by Ecclesiastes 11:3: "If a tree falls to the south or to the north, in the place where the tree falls, there it will lie." I was engaged in a conversation about wisdom with a Christian man, and I was coming from the perspective of a skeptic.

At that time in my life, I was going through a period of melancholy and dejection that was generated by a sense of the futility of my life and of human existence. Of course, this is what led him to talk to me about the book of Ecclesiastes and its well-known refrain "Vanity of vanities! All is vanity." Vanity here is meant not in the sense of pride but in the sense of futility. The question being addressed in Ecclesiastes is that of the apparent futility of human existence. The literature of the ancient world commonly explored this most basic of all questions: Is there any meaning or purpose to life and existence? The author of Ecclesiastes looks at all these points of passion, frustration, and skepticism that assault us in our daily lives.

When this man shared the words of Ecclesiastes 11:3, it was like a sudden epiphany for me. The scales fell from my eyes, and I saw myself as a tree that had fallen—lying on the floor of the forest, absolutely inert, producing nothing, in a state of rottenness and decay, and unable to reroot itself and bring forth fruit. It was as though my whole life passed before me, and I saw myself as a dead, rotting tree on the floor of the forest. God spoke to me through that text when I was in the position of despair that is addressed in Ecclesiastes with the deepest words of divine wisdom.

In this book, we see an early form of apologetics in the answers to the existential questions raised by skeptics and enemies of the Christian faith.

The next book, sometimes called the Canticle, is more popularly known as the Song of Songs or the Song of Solomon. It is famous for its rich imagery of love and romance. For example, in chapter 4 we read, "Behold, you are beautiful, my love, behold, you are beautiful! Your eyes are doves behind your veil. Your hair is like a flock of goats leaping down the slopes of Gilead" (v. 1). In ancient days, the image of black goats descending a green mountainside was a beautiful sight to the people. They would see someone with beautiful, flowing, black hair—rich and deep like the color of these goats—and they would say, "Your hair reminds me of a flock of goats moving down the slopes of Gilead." That was a compliment, not an insult.

Further on, the writer says,

Your teeth are like a flock of shorn ewes
    that have come up from the washing,
all of which bear twins,
    and not one among them has lost its young.
Your lips are like a scarlet thread,

and your mouth is lovely.
Your cheeks are like halves of a pomegranate
    behind your veil.
Your neck is like the tower of David,
    built in rows of stone;
on it hang a thousand shields,
    all of them shields of warriors.
Your two breasts are like two fawns,
    twins of a gazelle,
    that graze among the lilies. . . .
. . . You are altogether beautiful, my love;
    there is no flaw in you. (vv. 2–7)

In chapter 2, the writer of the Song uses this language:

I am a rose of Sharon,
    a lily of the valleys.

As a lily among brambles,
    so is my love among the young women.

As an apple tree among the trees of the forest,
    so is my beloved among the young men.

With great delight I sat in his shadow,
    and his fruit was sweet to my taste. (vv. 1–3)

Do you see how vivid and graphic the images of love used in the Song of Solomon are? No love song in all of history has ever transcended the beauty of this Canticle. One of the strange things about this book in church history is that it became a tradition in the Western church to interpret the Song of Solomon as an allegory of Christ's love for the church. The chief reason was that much of the imagery is so sensuous. It's not just about romantic love—there is an element of the erotic in it.

These are two people in love and looking forward to marriage and its sexual dimension. The church was somewhat embarrassed by the presence of this book in the canon of sacred Scripture. To evade this discomfort, they chose not to take the words literally and instead understood it as a symbolic presentation of a love that is absolutely pure and holy—the kind of love that we can only find in the relationship between Christ and His church.

Nothing in sacred Scripture indicates that the intent of the writing of Song of Solomon was to be an allegorical expression of the love of Christ for His church. It is certainly suitable to illustrate the purity of love that Christ has for the church and that the church should have for Christ—the Bridegroom and the bride—and we can certainly apply it illustratively to that relationship. But the fact remains that if this language is unsuitable to express a godly relationship between human beings, it would be even more unsuitable to apply it to a relationship between Christ and the church. It is best to understand it as it was intended—as a Spirit-inspired expression of shameless love between a man and a woman, between a bride and her groom.

There is nothing wrong with being in love. There is nothing wrong with extolling the beauty of a wife or a husband. There is nothing wrong with the bridegroom's being attracted to his bride and having a physical desire for her. What is prohibited in Scripture is the exercise of that physical desire outside the covenant context of marriage. But the attraction itself is part of what brings them together in the first place, part of what they find so lovely about each other. There is much wrong with the romance that we experience in our culture, but the answer is not to flee to a monastery and deny the reality of the physical attraction between the sexes or the erotic element of marriage. Rather, the answer is to understand romance in a way that is pleasing to God. If you want to know what real love is, spend some time in the Song of Solomon. It is a magnificent expression of romantic love.

The other book included in the category of Wisdom Literature is the book of Job. In one sense, Job is in a class by itself. The level of literary majesty found in this book is often underappreciated. The vocabulary is vivid and rich and extremely poetic.

What we find in Job is a lengthy, protracted drama set in patriarchal times. If ever there were such a thing as a morality play, the book of Job would certainly qualify, because there is a moral to this story. The drama begins with an opening scene in heaven, where a contest is launched. A challenge is brought before God by Satan, one of the leading characters in this drama. Satan comes into the presence of God after "going to and fro on the earth, and from walking up and down on it" (Job 1:7). God replies to Satan, "Have you considered my servant Job, that there is none like him on the earth, a blameless and upright man, who fears God and turns away from evil?" (v. 8). And Satan says: "Does Job fear God for no reason? Have you not put a hedge around him and his house and all that he has, on every side? You have blessed the work of his hands, and his possessions have increased in the land" (vv. 9–10). Job had incredible wealth, a large family, and health. He had everything a person could ever want. In other words, Satan says to God: "Of course Job is on Your side. Why wouldn't he be? You've given everything to him." Satan continues, "But stretch out your hand and touch all that he has, and he will curse you to your face" (v. 11).

God allows Satan to take all that belongs to Job except his life, and what ensues is a story of untold agony, torture, and suffering. First, Job's livestock are stolen by rustlers. His children perish. Everything that was important to him is taken away. Finally, he is smitten by horrible sores and boils. He sits on a dung heap, using shards of pottery to scrape his own skin. He's in abject misery. While he is in the midst of all this drama, his friends come to console him.

These friends are convinced that Job must have committed evil for God to have visited him with such great pain and suffering, yet Job is not aware of any such sins. The comfort and consolation his friends come with is mixed with judgment, arrogance, and error. They've bought into the fatal assumption this book addresses: that every person's suffering is in direct proportion to his sin. We know that Job was more upright, comparatively speaking, than any of his friends, yet he suffered far more than they did. The question being addressed here is found throughout the Wisdom Literature: Why do the wicked prosper and the righteous suffer?

Job's friends provide no adequate answer and no real consolation. Job's wife, who can't stand to see her husband enduring such shame and pain, gives him this advice: "Curse God and die" (2:9). After this, Job curses the day of his birth: "Let the day perish on which I was born, and the night that said, 'A man is conceived'" (3:3). Job believes he'd be far better off never to have lived than to endure such pain.

How does Job respond? "Though he slay me, I will hope in him" (13:15). Job has no understanding whatsoever about why he was brought into this terrible torment. The only hope he has is to trust in God. Job then turns his fist toward heaven and demands a response from God. Job asks many theological questions, and when God finally appears to him, He never answers his questions. Instead, He interrogates Job in chapters 38–41.

God overwhelms Job with His power and majesty, and yet in that, there is an answer. The answer is God Himself. God doesn't tell Job why he suffers, but He says, "Here I am, Job. Look at Me, learn of Me, know who I am. That's all you need to know. If you know who I am, you can trust Me even now." And Job replies, "I had heard of you by the hearing of the ear, but now my eye sees you; therefore I despise myself, and repent in dust and ashes" (42:5–6). His heart surrenders in trust to God when there's no reason other than the manifestation of God Himself. Then the story ends with Job receiving blessings far and above what he ever had received before, and in this great piece of Wisdom Literature, the righteousness of God is vindicated and the hope of the world remains intact.

How precious and valuable authentic wisdom is, and how few there are who find it. We say sometimes that experience is the best teacher, but that's not the best source of wisdom. The best source of wisdom is the mind of God, and the Wisdom Literature is given to us that we might live, that we might know how to endure and respond to the exigencies that occur in our human existence. This world is a vale of tears, and pain and suffering come to every life. When they come, do we act like fools or do we search for the wisdom of God? He's given us a present, a gift of the substance of His wisdom, in these books called Wisdom Literature.

About the Author

Dr. R.C. Sproul was the founder of Ligonier Ministries, founding pastor of Saint Andrew's Chapel in Sanford, Fla., first president of Reformation Bible College, and executive editor of *Tabletalk* magazine. His radio program, *Renewing Your Mind,* is still broadcast daily on hundreds of radio stations around the world and can also be heard online. He was the author of more than one hundred books, including *The Holiness of God, Chosen by God,* and *Everyone's a Theologian.* He was recognized throughout the world for his articulate defense of the inerrancy of Scripture and the need for God's people to stand with conviction upon His Word.

Free eBooks *by* R.C. Sproul

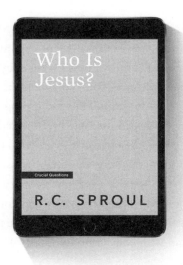

Does prayer really change things? Can I be sure I'm saved? Dr. R.C. Sproul answers these important questions, along with more than thirty others, in his Crucial Questions series. Designed for the Christian or thoughtful inquirer, these booklets can be used for personal study, small groups, and conversations with family and friends. Browse the collection and download your free digital ebooks today.

 Ligonier.org/freeCQ

ASK LIGONIER

Do we have free will?

Is it true that God controls everything?

Does prayer change things?

A Place to Find Answers

Maybe you're leading a Bible study tomorrow. Maybe you're just beginning to dig deeper. It's good to know that you can always ask Ligonier. For more than fifty years, Christians have been looking to Ligonier Ministries, the teaching fellowship of R.C. Sproul, for clear and helpful answers to biblical and theological questions. Now you can ask those questions online as they arise, confident that our team will work quickly to provide clear, concise, and trustworthy answers. The *Ask Ligonier* podcast provides another avenue for you to submit questions to some of the most trusted pastors and teachers who are serving the church today. When you have questions, just ask Ligonier.

FOR MORE INFORMATION, VISIT ASK.LIGONIER.ORG